The Backyard Homestead:

Growing and Feeding Your Chickens and

Best Beekeeping Tips

Table of content:

Backyard Chickens For Beginners

Build Your Own Chicken Coop, Learn To Feed & Care Naturally

Micheal Peal

Backyard Chickens For Beginners

Build Your Own Chicken Coop, Learn To Feed & Care Naturally

Introduction

Raising chickens in your backyard comes with many rewards! Of course, the greatest rewards are eggs. Eggs that your chickens can produce are nutritionally better for your health than those you can buy in stores. These eggs simply burst with healthy fats, carotene, omega-3, and vitamins A and E. Fresh and healthy eggs are a perfect way to start off your day, and plus, when you know that this is your own product and that it is 100% healthy, you will enjoy even more.

All those annoying backyard pests, such as insects, mosquitoes, flies, and bugs will run away from your garden because they will know that the moment they come there it will be dinner time for your chickens. So, if you have a garden and love to spend some time there, your chickens will make sure that you have a pleasant time without having to fight with mosquitoes and flies. It's a win-win situation because your chickens will be fed as well.

What is even more, the plants in your garden will love chicken litter. You can combine chicken litter with compost and make a perfect fertilizer that will make your garden bloom in no time.

It may sound strange to you, but chickens are actually great pets. As you will take care of them since they are little puffy balls, they will create a special bond with you.

So, don't be surprised when they run to you when they see you in the morning or if they jump to you to cuddle. Once you let chickens in your life, they will really quickly become loved members of your family. The beginning demands a lot of time and care, though. But once you have your grown-up chickens, all the rewards will come quickly.

However, there is one thing to consider before starting this adventure. Living in a rural area is a great thing if you want to start raising chicken. However, in case you want to do urban or suburban chicken-keeping, then there are some important things to check if you want to avoid problems. So, first check what the regulations are in your area regarding chicken-keeping. For instance, in some areas, there is a limit on the number of chickens whereas in some others keeping roosters is forbidden because of the noise they make.

To help you get started with making important decisions and preparations for these lovely creatures, go on reading and learn how to become a great chicken parent.

Chapter 1 – Choose Your Breed

Picking the right breed can make a difference between enjoying every moment you spend with your chickens and questioning why you wanted chickens in the first place. And this is especially true for beginner chicken parents.

Depending on the breed, chickens will show different qualities. For instance, some are great egg layers, some are flighty, whereas some are very cuddly and calm. Here are the things to think about when you choose chickens for you and your family.

NOTE: If it happens that you choose the one you think is the best for you and it turns out that after a year or so you are not quite satisfied, then don't worry, nothing is lost. Just pick another one and start from the beginning.

CHICKEN
breeds

1. Araucana (White) male. 2. Orpington (Blue) female. 3. Jersey Giant (Black) male. 4. Sussex Bantam (Light) female. 5. Araucana (Blue) female. 6. Poland (White) female. 7. Wyandotte Bantam (Silverlaced) female. 8. Poland (White Crested Black) female. 9. Naked Neck (Black) male. 10. Old English Game Bantam (Pilezeous) female. 11. Gingernut Ranger female. 12. Plymouth Rock (Barred) male. 13. Ancona (Rose Comb) female. 14. Brahma (Dark) male. 15. Hamburgh / Holland Fowl (Silver Spangled) male. 16. Cochin (Buff) male. 17. Frisée Bantam (White) female. 18. Friesian (Yellow Pencilled) female. 19. Pekin Bantam (White) male. 20. Faverolle (Salmon) male. 21. Houdan (Black Mottled) female. 22. Wyandotte Bantam (Blue) male. 23. Old English Game (Grey) male. 24. Barbu d'Anvers (Buff) male. 25. Appenzeller Spitzhauben (Silver Spangled) female. 26. Minorca (Black) female. 27. Barbu de Watermael (Quail) female. 28. Old English Game Bantam (Wheaten) female. 29. Old English Pheasant Fowl (Gold) female. 30. Poland (Chamois) male. 31. Silkie (White) female. 32. Malay (Wheaten) female. 33. Dorking (Silver Grey) male. 34. Brahma Bantam (Dark) male. 35. Pekin Bantam (Mottled) male. 36. Scots Dumpy (Cuckoo) male. 37. Barbara (Black & White) female. 38. Cochin (Blue) female. 39. Sussex (Light) male. 40. Ko Shamo (Black Red) male. 41. Nankin (Buff) female. 42. Yokohama (White) female. 43. Brahma Bantam (Light) female. 44. Asil (Dark Red) male. 45. Rosecomb Bantam (Black) female. 46. Silkie (Black) male. 47. Orpington (Buff) male. 48. Barbu d'Uccle (Porcelain) female. 49. La Fleche (Black) female. 50. Japanese Bantam (Black-Tailed White) male. 51. Indian Game (Jubilee) female. 52. Nankin (Buff) male. 53. Houdan (Black Mottled) female. 54. Rooted Bantam (White) female. 55. Sicilian Buttercup (Gold) male. 56. Appenzeller Spitzhauben (Silver Spangled) male.

Egg Size, Productivity & Color

You have probably decided to raise chickens because of eggs. With that in mind, it is probably good to go with hybrids, such as the California, Hy-Line Brown, Cherry Egger, Golden Comet, and Indian River. On the other hand, if you prefer heritage breeds, you may choose White-Faced Black Spanish, Leghorns, Australorps, Rhode Island Reds, Plymouth Rocks, and Rhode Island Whites, as they are known as breeds that produce a lot of eggs.

When it comes to the size of eggs, the breeds to mention here include mostly hybrid breeds such as Golden Comets, Hy-Line Browns, Cinnamon Queens, and ISA Browns. As for heritage breeds, the breeds that produce the largest eggs are Australorps, Jersey Giants, Orpingtons, Plymouth Rocks, and Rhode Island Reds.

Another thing you should think about is how fast you want your chickens to start laying eggs. Different breeds need different time to mature. But if you are impatient and want to have fresh eggs on your table as soon as possible, then you should go with some hybrid breeds such as Indian Rivers, Cherry Eggers, Pearl Leghorns, ISA Browns, and Golden Comets. These generally mature quickly and can start laying eggs when they are only 17 weeks old. On the other hand, if you are looking for other heritage breeds, you can choose White-Faced Black Spanish, Red Caps, Minorcas, and Anconas. These breeds usually mature and start laying eggs when they are 21 weeks old.

The color of eggs can vary as well, and some people take this as one of the criteria when they choose breeds. Well, most breeds lay eggs whose eggshell color vary from white to orange and yellow. But if you would like your chickens to lay brown eggs, then you can decide to go with the breeds such as Barnevelders, Marans, and Welsummers. There are some breeds, such as Ameraucanas and Araucanas that lay eggs of bluish or greenish color.

You have probably heard a lot about free-range chickens and maybe you are into it or you are not sure what exactly you want. If you are still thinking whether or not you want free-range eggs, it is probably better to choose breeds that can live equally well both on free range and in confinement. Such breeds are Cornish, Langshans, Houdans, Polish, and Pearl Leghorn.

When you start raising your own chickens, you should be aware of the fact that some breeds, such as Leghorns, can be nervous or flighty. Even though they are good egg producers, they can make raising chickens a nightmare for you, especially if you don't have any previous experience. So, choose some breeds that are easy to manage and calm, such as Brahmas, Faverolles, Silkies, Orpingtons, and Cochins.

What Weather Do Chickens Like?

When choosing a perfect breed for you, it is also good to think about the weather. Maybe this doesn't sound like an important element, but it actually is. What is even more, it can make daily maintenance easier and your flock healthier. So, if you live in a cold climate, then good choices for you are Buckeyes, Chanteclers, Javas, and Brahmas. On the other hand, the best breeds for hot weather are Cubalayas, Sumatras, Jungle Fowl, Javas, and Malays.

What Breeds Are Naturally Good Mothers?

When you get your first little flock, you may not think that you want to make it bigger. But soon when you get into taking care of chickens, you will want to have more. So, maybe you can think about this as well when you choose the breed for yourself. In this case, you should know that some breeds are naturally good at raising chicks such as Aseels, Silkies, Old English Games, Modern Games, and Cochins. Most hens of these breeds are also good foster mothers, which means that they will also hatch eggs from other breeds that you raise.

Where to Find Chickens?

The next step after choosing a breed is to look for places such as farm stores, local or online hatcheries. There are pros and cons of all of these. For instance, most farm stores sell only straight-run chicks, which means that you are not sure if you will get a hen or a rooster. So, if you want to be sure that you get hens, you should look for sexed chicks, which means that they are determined to be hens from the birth. Usually, they are labeled as pullets.

A good thing about online hatcheries is that you can choose the exact breed and get only pullets. However, the shipping process is stressful for both the birds and you. Thus, the best option for you will probably be a local hatchery. If you don't know there is any, just ask around and you'll find some for sure.

Chapter 2 – Build Your Brooder

Taking care of these little fluffy balls is simple. You just have to keep an eye on them and give them good quality starter food. Another important thing is to spend time with them, which won't be hard because they are all so cute and puffy. Interacting with them while they are young will sort of tame them so that when they grow up they will feel comfortable around you. But for the beginning, you will need your own brooder.

How to Set Up a Brooder

Simply put, a brooder is a confined area that provides a safe and warm environment for young chicks. Nowadays, you can buy brooders, but you can also make your own since it won't take you much time.

The easiest thing you can do is find a cardboard box because you can easily change it when it becomes soggy. Other things you can use are plastic storage boxes or deep wooden crates. Whichever of these you choose, make sure that the chicks have enough room. Keep an eye on the chicks since they develop quickly because you'll have to change the brooder so that they have enough space to move freely. You want to avoid overcrowding because it may lead to stress-related problems and disease.

Once you choose a brooder that is perfect for the little chicks, it would be a good idea that you cover it with a wired mesh. This way, you will keep them protected from curious pets (if you have them), but you will also be sure that the chicks don't go out of the brooder. You'll be amazed to see them jumping high as they try out their wings only after a few days.

Do You Need a Brooding Enclosure?

Since you are a beginner, it is recommended to start with a smaller number of birds. However, if you are enthusiastic or you just couldn't resist those cute fluffy chicks and already bought many, then a simple cardboard box won't be a good place for the chicks. Instead, you will definitely need a brooding enclosure.

To make this one, you will need some plastic brooding panels, a brooding ring, and pieces of cardboard that you will tape together. Once again, when the chicks start growing, and they grow fast, they will easily escape the enclosure.

Don't give them such opportunities and make the sides of the enclosure high. When chicks are still little, restrict the area of the brooder to keep them close to the food and heat. As they grow bigger and become more active, increase the space.

Where Should You Put the Brooder?

If you have a small flock, then a quiet room is a nice place for a brooder. The chicks will also need light that will help their development but keep in mind that they also need a few hours of darkness when they sleep at night.

The brooder can also be placed outside or even in the coop if you have already built it. However, it is of utmost importance that the place where you keep your chicks is rat-proof. Rats will be attracted by the smell and will kill the chicks if they have an access to them.

How to Keep the Chicks Warm?

Since the chicks will need light, there should either be a good source of natural light or power for the heat lamp. However, there should also be an unheated spot where chicks can eat and drink.

When setting up your brooder, pay special attention that the heat lamp is fixed securely above it. One option is to attach it to a chain which is attached to a ceiling hook. Another thing you can do is suspend the lamp on a wheeled clothing rail. It would be really disastrous if the lamp falls on the chicks or if it is too close to them. If you use a cardboard box for your brooder, make sure that the lamp is at a safe distance from it. These traditional lamps may get really hot and even pose a fire hazard. As the chicks get bigger week by week, you should not forget to decrease the heat. To do that, simply raise the lamp (or lower it to increase the heat).

Besides traditional lamps, there are also special panel heaters that you can buy and that offer the closest alternative to natural brooding. Generally, these panels are safer, as they don't get as hot as traditional lamps. Moreover, they have their own stands, which means that you don't have to hang them as lamps, and for some people, this is more convenient.

These panels warm only the space underneath them as opposed to traditional lamps which heat a wider area. Although heater panels have their advantages, they are a bit more expensive, so if you have just started your journey of being a chicken parent, then you can first try with traditional lamps which basically do the same job. You will just have to be more careful with them.

You can also use a thermometer to check the temperature, but it is actually not that necessary. Just keep your eye on the chicks, and based on their behavior, you'll see if the temperature is pleasant to them. If they huddle together, then it definitely means that they are cold. If on the other hand, they move away from the heat or they pant, then it means that the temperature is too high for them.

Drinkers & Feeders

Some other things you will need for your brooder are drinkers and feeders. Both the feeder and drinker should not be placed too high because if the chicks have to stretch to reach water and food, there are chances that they will have some developmental problems. The feeder and drinker should always be kept outside of the heated area.

What to Use for Bedding & Food?

For the bedding, dust-extracted shavings may be a good choice but, at the same time, they can be dangerous because small chicks can eat them. So, for the first several days you can use paper towels. Newspapers are also a practical solution but again, it is better to avoid them until chicks are a couple of weeks old. Newspapers can be slippery and that can lead to chicks with splayed legs.

As for the food, chicks will mostly enjoy chicken crumbs, so make sure you stock up on these.

Prepare Your Brooder

Before you start using it, the brooder should be thoroughly cleaned and disinfected. Then, cover the floor with a good layer of bedding. If you use a cardboard box, it may be a good idea to first cover the floor with an additional layer of cardboard which will absorb excess moisture. The next thing to do is to set your panel heater or a lamp. Get your drinker and feeder ready, prepare chick crumbs and wait for the eggs to hatch.

Chapter 3 – Build The Coop

Having cute baby chicks in your brooder means that you will have to build a proper home for them soon because they can't live in a cardboard box forever. The very first thought of building a chicken coop on your own may look intimidating. But if you are determined, it will turn out to be a one-week project in case you want a basic coop for a small flock of birds. If on the other hand, you want to build a fancy, more elaborate coop, then you'll need more than a week, plus some advanced carpentry skills.

Whatever option you choose, your chicken coop will have two basic parts – an enclosed area where the birds will sleep and lay eggs and an open area where chickens will spend most of the day roaming around.

This enclosed area should be elevated two or more feet so that you can collect the eggs that will fall through the floor. Anyway, there are many different ways to plan your chicken coop, but here is one basic plan, together with the step-by-step instructions, that you can easily change and adjust to fit your taste and needs.

Plan the Size & Choose the Location

Start by considering the size. Let this be your guideline: the minimum space per bird is 2 to 3 square feet for the enclosed area and 4 to 5 square feet for the open area. These are the minimum requirements but it is not set in stone. So, if you have extra space, feel free to plan a bigger coop than necessary. On the contrary, it is not recommended to make a smaller coop because if the coop is overcrowded, you'll find your chickens squabbling frequently.

As for the location, try to find a space with a large deciduous tree. This would be ideal for chickens because it will create a shade in summer, and in winter, when the leaves fall off, chickens can bask in the sun.

If you don't have such a spot, no worries. You will just have to use shade cloth to shade the open area during summer.

What Materials to Prepare

As for the materials, you should try to find lumber that is naturally resistant to rotting, such as redwood and cedar. On the other hand, you can also find pressure treated lumber, but this is not a good choice because it may contain heavy metals that may be harmful to your chickens.

Moreover, you will need to get metal chicken mesh to cover the open area and protect your chickens from predators. And finally, some galvanized gate hinges and nails, screws, and bailing wire will also be needed.

Start Building the Coop

Step 1: Set 4x4 vertical posts in concrete to form the rectangular shape you chose for the coop. The front posts should be 8 feet tall whereas the back ones should be 6 feet tall.

Step 2: Locate the spot 2 feet away from the right front corner. Add one 4x4 post there; it should be 8 feet tall and it will support the entryway to the open area of the coop.

Step 3: Take a 2x4 post and screw it horizontally between the posts mentioned in Step 2; to screw the post, locate the height of 6 feet on the right front of the open area.

Step 4: You can now build the gate frame that should fit the space of the gateway. The size of this rectangle should be 2x6. As for the materials, use 2x2 lumber and screw or nail the posts together.

If necessary, to prevent the gate frame from sagging, you can use an anti-sag gate kit. Once you have the frame finished, use galvanized gate hinges to attach it to the corner post.

Step 5: Now you can move on and work on the enclosed area. So, locate the position that is about 1/3 of the distance from the left side corner posts and add two parallel 4x4 posts. The height of the posts should be the same as the height of the other front and back posts. This way, you will support the frame of the enclosed area.

Step 6: When you finish that, take a look at all the front and back posts of the coop frame. Now you should attach a frame of horizontal 2x4 posts between the tops of all these posts. Moreover, you will have to add three more of these at an angle between the three pairs of the front and back posts, and these will be rafters.

Step 7: Go to the left side of the coop frame, locate the four posts there and attach a frame of horizontal 2x4 posts. The frame should be attached 24 inches above the ground. These frames are to support the floor of the enclosed area.

Step 8: Now you can add the floor planks on top of the front 2/3 of this 2x4 frame. Use decking screws or galvanized nails to attach the planks.

Step 9: Measure out chicken wire and use it to cover the remaining 1/3 of the floor. Since your chickens will use this part for roosting, the droppings will fall through the hardware cloth so that they can be collected from below.

Step 10: The basic frame of the coop is almost finished. You just have to make sure that your chickens will be protected against digging animals. So, go to the open area of the coop and dig a trench around the perimeter of the area. It should be approximately 12 inches deep.

Take chicken wire and stretch it between the posts of the open area on the right 2/3 of the frame. Stretch it vertically between the posts to form walls and horizontally to form the ceiling. To attach the chicken wire to the posts, use poultry staples. The chicken wire should go all the way to the bottom of the trenches. Once you do this, fill the trenches again with soil in order to keep the wire in place.

Step 11: Use chicken wire to cover the gate frame as well.

NOTE: Take a look at the diagram below to get a better idea of how the coop should look like.

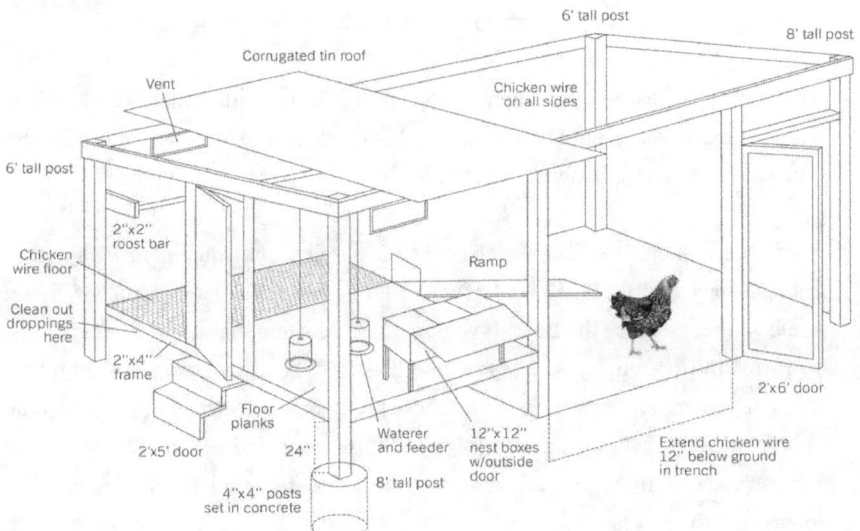

Work on the Interior

There is actually not much to be done for the open area. You will just have to cover the ground with a thick layer of straw that will absorb the moisture during rainy days or of chicken droppings.

It is also recommended to add one watering device that will hang some 6-8 inches from the ground. You can attach it to one of the rafters using bailing wire.

In case this open area doesn't get any shade, you should definitely think about adding a piece of cloth on top of the ceiling. This will protect your chickens from hot weather.

And the last thing for the open area is a ramp that the chickens will use to go from the enclosed area to the open one and vice versa. This ramp is nothing more than a wooden plank wide approximately 8 inches. Just set the plank so that it goes from the enclosed platform to the ground level.

The enclosed area will need some more things to be added there. First, add a roosting 2x2 bar along the back wall over the chicken wire floor. As for the length, you will need at least 8 inches per bird.

Then, there should be some nest boxes. Generally, one square, 12-inch box is enough for 3-4 birds. The nest boxes should be placed along the front wall and some 24 inches above the floor. If you don't feel like making your own nest boxes, you can find prefabricated ones or use plastic kitty litter boxes. On the other hand, if you are enthusiastic to build these boxes on your own, you can use some simple wooden shelves, add some plywood to serve as dividers, and fill the boxes with straw. One thing to think about is that the nest boxes should be positioned lower than the roosts.

Since chickens will always try to find the highest places in a coop, if you place the nest boxes high and your chickens start using them for roosting, nests will quickly become soiled.

And finally, you will need a feeder and a watering device. They can be attached to the rafters with bailing wire so that they hang some 6-8 inched above the ground.

The Final Steps

The open area is finished, so you just need to finish the enclosed area and your coop will be ready for its inhabitants. So, the walls and roof are still missing. For this purpose, you can use any waterproof material. (Additional 2x4 framing will be necessary for the walls and roof structure).

However, an important thing to note here is that you should not forget to plan access to clean the coop and collect eggs. To make sure these access points are raccoon-proof, use a regular gate latch with a carabineer in the turnbuckle.

It is recommended to have access on three sides. So, you will need a door where you will set the ramp that goes from the enclosed area to the open one. As for the size, 12x12 inches is usually enough for this door.

At the front wall, there should be an access to collect eggs. The size should be 12x12 inch hatches.

And to get to clean the coop and access the feeder and water, a 2x5 foot door to the left wall is good for it.

To construct these access doors, a simple 2x2 frame will be sufficient. Make these in the same way as the main gate frame that you will use as the entrance to the open area.

For covering these frames, use the same material you used for covering the closed area of the coop. You will not need to use the anti-sag kit for these frames.

And the most important thing is ventilation, especially in summer. The part of the floor in the closed area covered with the chicken mesh, as well as the main door will let in air. However, hot air will have to have a way to go out of the coop. To make these vents, just leave a space between the eaves of the roof or cut some vents near the top of the walls. As always, make sure that your chickens are protected from animals, so cover these vents with chicken wire.

Take a look at the diagram of the finished coop below. Once again, this is a basic coop, but feel free to modify it any way you like.

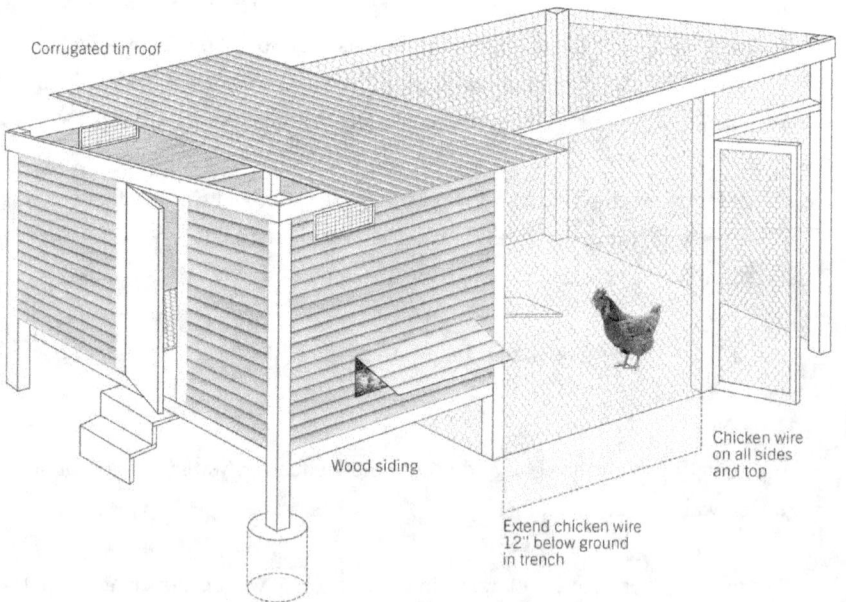

Corrugated tin roof

Wood siding

Chicken wire
on all sides
and top

Extend chicken wire
12″ below ground
in trench

Moving Your Chicks to the Coop

Once your chicks are around 5 to 6 weeks old, you can start moving them to their coop. Basically, this is the time when they are no longer fluffy but have a full set of feathers that can keep them warm while outside.

Now, if you are concerned about how your chickens will accept the new home, you don't have to worry that much. Some chicken parents keep their chickens locked up in the coop for several days to give them time to adapt and accept the coop as their safe home. Moreover, you can place some dummy eggs in nest boxes, which will show chickens that they should use these for laying eggs.

Chapter 4 – Learn To Feed Your Chickens

Feeding your chicken properly will result in having fresh and healthy eggs all year round. It is actually very straightforward once you know how and what you should feed them. A diet that is good for chicken is a high-quality poultry pellet. This type of food generally contains salt, wheat, sunflower seeds, maize, and oats and thus provides chickens with the necessary proteins and minerals that will keep them healthy and make them lay eggs.

Additionally, you can feed your chicken grains such as wheat or corn. Chickens also love vegetables and fruits, so you can feed them these daily. You can also try feeding them with broccoli, carrots, apple cores, bananas, and vegetable peels. However, avoid raw green peels, such as green potato peels, as well as fruits such as lemons and oranges.

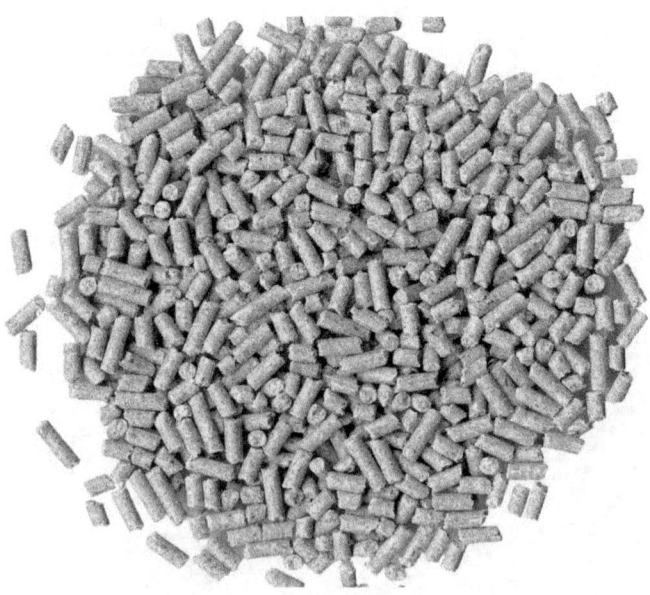

How To Feed Chickens

Chickens like to eat smaller portions but like to enjoy food often. So, you can feed them pellets once in the morning and once in the evening. As for the amount of food, well, you will have to try and see how much your chickens eat. Basically, the amount of food they need depends on the breed, on how active your chickens are during the day, as well as on the time of the year. Chickens won't overeat; if you give them more food than they can eat, they will just leave it. However, bear in mind that you should not leave any food overnight because it may attract mice and other pests.

When you feed your chickens, maybe you will notice that some of them are more aggressive and eat more than the others. If that is the case in your coop, then think about feeding those weaker chickens separately.

As for the water, just make sure that your chickens always have clean and fresh water.

How to Know If Their Diet Is Not Right

And, one last thing to mention is to observe your chickens' behavior. It can change if the diet is not good for them. For instance, if the egg production has reduced or you have noticed some general unrest and feather pecking in the coop, it may be a sign that there is something wrong with their diet. An even clearer sign are abnormal eggs; more precisely, if you notice that your chickens lay eggs with double yolks or the eggs are too small, then you should think about changing their diet.

Conclusion

Here you have found your complete guide to raising your own backyard chickens. The book leads you from the very first steps of choosing the right breed for you through setting up a brooder and building a coop to the detailed instructions on how to feed and take care of your chicken. As a result, your chickens will reward you with fresh and nutritious eggs every day. Enjoy your chicken parenting!

Kristen Towne

Beekeeping

Step-by-Step Guide
For Beginner and
Advanced Beekeepers

Beekeeping:

Step-By-Step Guide For Beginner And Advanced Beekeepers

Introduction

We have all heard of the land that is flowing with milk and honey, and when we close our eyes, we think of how wonderful that would be. To have as much honey as you want, when you want – it's more than just a dream, it would make your life much easier.

There are many benefits to adding honey into your diet regularly, from fighting off viruses and infections to slimming down and keeping the weight off. When it comes to honey, all you can see are the good, as there is very little bad.

But, honey is expensive. You have shopped around, you have tried to find the best you can get without breaking the bank, but you are consistently coming home with a small jar and an empty wallet. You have to ration to ensure that you are getting your money's worth out of the sweet substance, but you know that ultimately you could be going about this better.

But how? You can't go out into the woods and find a beehive now, could you? Not only is it difficult to find a honey hive, you would have to put up with the stings of thousands of bees who are all willing to die for the sake of their hive.

No, instead, you are going to have to go about this in another way.
You are going to have to keep your own bees.

Wait a minute, you think, how are you going to pull that off? Isn't keeping bees difficult? How do you make sure they are warm enough in the winter, and don't abandon the hive in the summer? Where do you even get bees to begin with?

With all these questions, it's easy to feel overwhelmed, but don't worry. If you are serious about starting your own beehive and beekeeping career, you have come to the right place.

I am going to show you everything you need to know to start – and maintain – your beekeeping hobby, and give you the secret to harvesting honey whenever you like.

This book is going to revolutionize the way you think about bees, and how you get your honey. By the time you reach the end, you are going to realize just how sweet this deal is.

Let's get started.

Chapter 1 – An Introduction to Beekeeping

If this is your first time beekeeping, it is likely that you are going to have a lot of questions. Odds are, you have seen beehives in farms or in fields before, though they are often too far away for you to see the bees themselves. Perhaps you have been fortunate enough to visit with friends or relatives who also keep bees, and you have been able to see the hives close up.

Unless you have engaged in beekeeping yourself in the past, now is the time to really get familiar with the hobby before you dive in.

People have been gathering honey since the dawn of time. With great skill (and a high pain tolerance) mankind has been known to have gathered honey for nearly 10,000 years. However, there is documented proof that Egyptians have domesticated and harvest bee honey for nearly 5000 years.

Though back in ancient times getting honey from bees was a more difficult task, modern day beekeeping needs to be well-researched, and you should really know what you are getting yourself in to before you begin. If bees are unhappy in their hive, or if they feel that they are in danger, they will swarm and find somewhere else to live, leaving you back at square one.

With this in mind, it is important that you know how to care for your bees before you bring them into the picture, so you can ensure they like the hive you prepare for them, and choose to stay there.

To start, it is important that you check into the local ordinances of where you live, and determine whether you need a permit for your hive or not. It's rare to need a permit to keep bees, however, it does happen, and you don't want to set up a hive, only to have it taken from you or to get fined later because you didn't know you needed a permit.

Next, understand that bees have their flight patterns, and that they are often follow the same routes when they are out gathering pollen. Their brains are wired to memorize maps of where the food is, and they will return to the same location day after day, gathering pollen and nectar to bring back to the hive (and turn into honey.)

With this in mind, place the hive in an area where the bees' flight pattern won't disturb your family, neighbors, or pets. Bees are very busy creatures, and they would rather not have to engage in any kind of activity with anyone other than the other members of the hive – so doing this is just as much a favor to them as it is to you.

Is beekeeping a lot of work?

The amount of work you put into beekeeping is going to vary. This is an incredibly seasonal hobby, meaning you are going to have virtually nothing to do in the winter, and you might find that it occupies all your free time in the spring. When it comes to bees, you are going to be in charge of the basic care, then let them handle the rest. Of course, you are going to get involved when it comes time to harvest the honey, but realize that bees are incredibly self-sufficient, and the less you are involved, the better.

When it comes to effective beekeeping, strategy is the best policy. Understand what a bee colony is and how it functions, understand the level of work you are going to have to put forth to ensure that your colony thrives, and understand how little (or how much) you are going to be involved to ensure that it is a success.

Learn how much honey you are allowed to take from the bees at a time, and remember to be generous with them when it comes to their honey. Only take what they have to spare and no more than that. There are a lot of rules that you need to follow, but trust me, once you get the hang of things, you are going to be set with your beekeeping hobby.

Time, diligence, and dedication are the three ingredients to beekeeping success.

Chapter 2 – Understanding the Colony

To ensure that you are going to give the bees everything they need, it is important that you understand what the colony is, and how it works. Though they may just seem like worker bees and a queen to us, there is actually an intricately designed system that is taking place, and each bee knows where they fit into that system.

Queen Bees

The queen bee is the only bee in the colony which lays fertilized eggs. Contrary to popular belief, she does not mate with the other bees throughout her lifetime, but rather, she mates early on in her life and stores the sperm within herself to continuously fertilize eggs throughout her life.

She is one of the most crucial parts to the colony, and without her, the colony will leave. Though it has been recorded that queen bees can live up to five years, a queen bee that is working hard to produce more eggs for the colony is more likely to live only two or three years before she passes on.

Colonies can grow to include thousands of bees – which is of little wonder when you learn that a queen bee can lay as many as two thousand eggs in just a single day.

Worker Bees

The queen bee lays the fertilized eggs in the colony, and when they hatch, they produce female worker bees. These bees are basically the backbone of the colony, converting the nectar that comes in with the other worker bees into honey, caring for the larvae, and making repairs around the colony as needed.

Though these worker bees can lay eggs, it is unusual for them to do so unless there is no queen present, or if the queen isn't producing as many eggs as she should be.

Drones

When there is no queen, or when the queen is unable to produce as many eggs as she ought, the worker bees will lay their unfertilized eggs, which then become the drones. The sole purpose of the drone is to fertilize the queen, and each male dies soon after mating.

It is not at all unusual for the worker bees in a colony to banish the male drones when the weather starts to cool, or when there is hardship in the colony. Though it is crucial that drones are in the picture from time to time, they really do place a small part in the activity of the colony as a whole, and are simply discarded by the rest of the bees when they have done their job.

Larvae

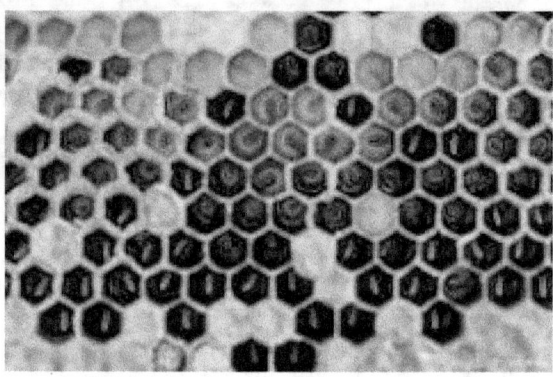

All bees begin as larvae, and undergo a scientific change which is known as metamorphosis. This is the process by which an egg is laid, then it is hatched into a larval. The larva then changes into a pupal, then they grow into their adult form.

A larval will shed its skin several times during this process before it finally emerges as an adult, and takes its place within the colony.

As I said, a colony is highly systematic, with each of the members doing what they are supposed to do and contributing to the good of the colony as a whole.

This is why it is important that you keep any interference with the colony to a minimum. Bees who are harassed tend to feel threatened, and they are willing to abandon a hive if it is for the overall good of the colony.

As the beekeeper, it is up to you to ensure that the main frame of the colony is taken care of, but as the beekeeper it is up to you to ensure that they are able to handle things for themselves.

Don't worry, I am going to show you how to care for your bees, and ensure both you – and they – are able to co-exist for a mutually beneficial relationship.

Chapter 3 – Getting Started the Right Way

The first step to successful beekeeping is to get what you need from the beginning. As I have already said, bees like to be left alone, and this means from the minute they are introduced to their new hive. You can plan on releasing the bees into the hive, then letting them get established on their own – something that you can imagine would be difficult if an intruder kept poking around.

So, to get started on the right track, you are going to have to ensure that you have all the supplies that you need before beginning.

This includes:

• **Hives – you can make these yourself using wood and other necessary supplies, or you can order kits that walk you through step by step –** For a first time beekeeper, I would recommend that you opt for a kit, as these are going to have everything you need (and in the proper size) for your bees.

• You can find these kits virtually anywhere, including online department stores, Amazon, or private sellers (who are also online.)

- **Proper clothing** – if you want to harvest your honey without getting stung, you are going to need to have the proper clothing to do so. If you are harvesting honey the right way, you aren't going to have to worry about getting stung anyway, but this is added resistance that will greatly aid in the comfort you feel when you are harvesting.

- **Get a smoker and a hive tool** – a smoker and a hive tool are going to be the two things you use during the harvest. The smoker is going to put the bees to sleep or calm them down enough that you can get into the hive without too much trouble, and the hive tool is going to be used in the collection of the honey itself.

- **Once you have all the necessary supplies, source and order your bees.**

It is a good idea to go with a reputable bee seller for this, and understand that your bees are going to come in the mail. Though they are going to come packaged, this is still completely safe, as they are going to be enclosed in screen.

Keep in mind that your bees are going to be alive – meaning that they are going to have to survive the journey. Order from as nearby as you can to ensure there is minimal processing time – even if you were to overnight the bees from the other side of the country they are going to go through a lot of stress before they are delivered.

A common order for bees includes one queen bee and about three pounds of worker bees. The queen is going to be in her own box, so she is going to be easy for you to find and separate from the rest. Often, the bees also come with sugar water to keep them fed and hydrated throughout their journey.

Once the bees arrive, don't waste any time in getting them out into the hive where they belong. Open the side of the hive, giving you access to the inside, and pour the bees in. Once you open the box the bees came in, they are going to begin crawling out. Don't panic, simply pour them into the hive.

To make this process easier, begin with pouring syrup over the bars on the inside of the hive. This is not only going to give the bees something to do with themselves while they are put into the hive, but it is also going to keep them calm.

You may have to shake the box to ensure all the bees come out of the hive. Make sure the box is empty before you discard. There is going to be a special place for you to keep the queen bee – but leave her in her box. You don't want the bees to leave, and until they are used to the area, they are going to be in danger of doing so.

They will get used to living where the queen lives, so make sure she adopts the hive as her own. As the worker bees eat away the food that is blocking her entrance, they are going to get used to her as being one of the colony, and she is going to get used to the hive as being her own.

Keep in mind that the queen bee is raised separately from the rest of the colony, meaning they are not going to recognize her as one of their own on the outset. If you were to just place her in the hive outside the box with the rest of the bees, it is likely that they would kill her thinking of her as a foreigner – and thus a threat – to the colony.

By the time the worker bees do release her from her box, she is going to have released enough pheromones that the hive simply accepts her as their own, meaning they are going to take over with the mating and egg laying, and you just have to wait.

Though it's up to the worker bees to free the queen from her box, it is up to you to make sure that this happens. She can't live in the box indefinitely, and it is ideal for her to be out of there within the first few days.

Give the hive a few days to get settled, then come back and check on it. The queen should hopefully be released within the first 4 days, but if you find that she is still in her box, then loosen the hole a bit so the bees find it easier to get her out of the box.

After loosening the box, place the box back in its place and let it sit another 24 hours. Come back and check once again, repeating the process until she had been freed from her box.

You will find that the bees are eager to get to work, and they are very smart with how to go about doing that. It is highly unlikely you are going to have any problem getting the queen free, and in no time at all they are going to be making their rounds and scouting for flowers to begin making honey.

During the first couple weeks, make sure you provide your bees with plenty of sugar water. They are going to be so caught up in adjusting to the hive and getting the queen out of her box they aren't going to have time to go and gather food for themselves.

As long as the bees are cared for and don't have anyone harassing them, you are going to find they settle in quickly.

Chapter 4 – Harvesting the Honey

Once the time comes to harvest the honey, you will see that your hard work and dedication has paid off. However, before you go running out into your backyard with a pale and a scraper, it's important to take a moment to know what to expect – and to get ready.

First of all, you should get dressed in the appropriate attire. Wear gloves, a veiled mask and secure boots at a minimum, though I highly recommend that you also don be-proof overalls to complete the outfit, especially if you are a beginner. If you went through and purchased the list of things I recommended, you should already have one of these suits handy and ready to slip on.

The first thing you are going to do is smoke the bees.

Approach the beehive from behind, waving the smoker in front of and around you and the hive, ensuring that it is well fumed. Place the smoker at the entryway to the hive, driving the bees further in. This should be done in a fluid, steady motion – don't jerk around or move in fast, short movements.

Gentle strides, showing you are self-assured is best for both you and the bees. Once the bees have calmed down and retreated within the lower levels of the hive, pry open the top. This is going to take some effort as bees coat everything in a thick, sticky substance to ensure it stays together.

Be patient with it and don't force it, gently pry it away until the top peels back and you are able to get inside.

Next, you are going to remove the bees from the hive.

You can do this in a variety of ways, from scraping them off (gently!) to using a bee blower that will blow them off (again, gently!) to using your hands to brush them away. Just make sure that the panels are free of any bees and you are ready to pull them out.

You should have a clean bucket ready and waiting, then pull out the panels one at a time, pushing the honey into the bucket, and replacing the panels once you have cleaned them. Again, this should be done in a fluid, self-assured motion.

As you will notice, you are going to have a lot of honeycomb mixed in the honey – you can get rid of this using an extractor.

An extractor is somewhat like a salad spinner in that it spins quickly, causing the honey to fly to the edge of the drum and drip down into the center spigot.

This is going to remove the combs from the honey, and ensure that you get the most for your hard work.

Bottle your honey next.

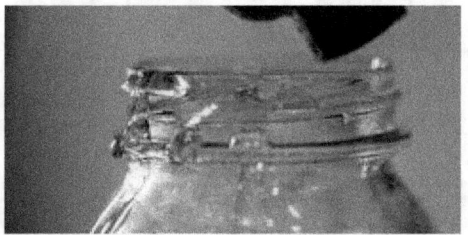

Make sure that you use honey that has been capped and matured by the bees – green honey is the newer batches, and though it might appear to be perfectly fine on the outside, it is actually prone to harboring yeast and bacteria and could cause your honey to spoil quickly – and once this happens, it is no longer safe for human consumption.

Now, many people question once they have harvested their honey whether they ought to then also pasteurize what they have gathered. This is a process that heats the honey to a high temperature, killing any potentially harmful bacteria or yeast which could be found in the honey.

While this is something that is entirely up to you to decide, it is important to note that doing this will also kill off some of the benefits that come with honey – so it's a decision you need to make for yourself.

Another thing to keep in mind when you are harvesting your honey is that it is always better to select quality honey over how much honey you are gathering, and it is important that you leave the bees with enough honey for themselves. There are many who keep bees who take more than they should, leaving the bees with a mix of sugar water or corn syrup – which the bees can't survive on.

Be fair with your portions, check the hives, and make sure everything is as it should be, and you are set!

Chapter 5 – Tips, Tricks, and Helpful Advice

That really is all you need to know to get started with your own beekeeping hobby – however, with as easy as it sounds, you must realize that it is going to take a lot of hard work for you to get your hive established and ready to go.

It's going to be worth it, and if you follow the methods that I have outlined here, you are going to have a thriving colony for years to come. However, even with the clearest of directions, there are still things you can do that will make this job that much easier, which is why I have included this final chapter of tips and tricks, plus some helpful advice that will make things run smoothly.

Try them out for yourself, and find what works for you – you just may be surprised.

Though bees are very much self-sufficient, when they are dealing with times of hardship, do your part and give them something to eat.

This can be syrup, sugar water, or candy – whatever works for you – just keep in mind that you should do this when the bees are having a hard time gathering enough nectar for themselves, not because you have taken too much of their honey.

As I said, working together with this relationship with your bees is the one thing that is going to ensure both of you are happy in the long run.

Feed your bees the syrups through a plastic bag to ensure they are able to reach the food, but they aren't going to fall in and drown.

To do this, you are going to fill a plastic Ziploc (or similar) bag with sugar water, syrup, or whatever it is you have chosen to use to feed your bees, then you are going to place it on the top rack in their hive. You are then going to take a sharp pair of scissors or a razor, and you are going to create slits along the top portion of the bag.

This will allow the bees to stand on top of the feeder without being in danger of falling in.

Don't forget the water.

In addition to their honey and the gathering that they do, the bees you keep are going to need water. Now, watering bees is rather tricky, as they are very picky about where they drink.

Try setting out a dog dish next to the hive and make sure to keep water in it at all times. Make sure any pets you have have another source of water so they aren't forced to go near the hive when they are in need of a drink.

If you have a problem with your bees swarming, trying replacing the queen every year.

Though many bees will be happy to reside in a certain hive for years, there are times when you may have a difficult time keeping your bees from leaving. This is because some bees enjoy swarming when the hive has grown strong, and they are always on the move for a new location with more food.

If you find that this keeps happening with your bees, simply replace the queen with a new, young queen every year. A queen that is less than a year old is going to provide plenty of eggs for the colony, but she is far less likely to swarm with the colony at her young age.

To introduce a young queen, you are going to follow the same steps that you did when you bought the bees in the first place. Be patient with them, and you are going to get the results that you want.

Put a fence around your hives.

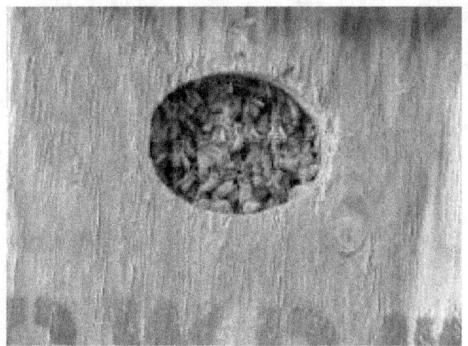

Ideally, this will be a six foot tall wooden fence or shrubbery, or something of that sort. This is going to force the bees to fly over everyone rather than through them, and it is going to make it less likely that anyone is going to bother your bees.

At the same time, it is going to give them protection from the wind, making it easier for them to come and go.

Try out all of these tricks regardless of how old your hive is, and you are going to have a successful colony (and a steady supply of honey) for years to come!

Conclusion

There you have it, everything you need to know to create your own bee colony, and how you can ensure they are going to be cared for and give you as much honey as you could ever use for years to come. I hope this book inspires you, whether you are a first time keeper or if you are adding on or starting up after a period of not expanding.

You are going to quickly learn that beekeeping is a hobby that is highly addictive, and regardless of how long you have been doing it, you will want to continue doing it and expanding your bees. The more bees you have, the stronger your colony is going to be, and the more honey you are going to get in the long run.

There really is no way you can ever complete this hobby, as you are going to start a cycle of caring for your bees and harvesting the honey – this will last as long as you want it to, and it will give you an organic, constant supply of the best honey on the planet.

You'll get to know your bees, and you will learn just how to care for them to ensure longevity and optimal care. If you pay attention to what you are doing, you really can't do it wrong, and this book is going to ensure that you get the help you need on the outset to guarantee the best results going forward.

It doesn't matter if this is your first colony or your hundredth, you are going to learn something new and useful here, giving you the boost you need to have a thriving colony for years to come. You are going to fall in love with not only the quality of the honey, but the process with which you get it.

Do what is right by your health, for your family, and for the planet, and you are going to see that organic, homegrown honey is truly the way to go. Your bees will thank you, and you will help preserve a species that is starting to face hardship.

Don't be afraid to put in the work, and you are going to be rewarded for your efforts, guaranteed. So gather the supplies you need, plan the work, then put your plan into action, and within months you are going to have that constant supply of honey you have been dreaming of.

Your health will increase, and your friends and family will thank you – trust me, it's not going to take long before you realize that this is all more than worth it. Good luck, and happy beekeeping.

www.ingramcontent.com/pod-product-compliance
Lightning Source LLC
Chambersburg PA
CBHW062023280526
45787CB00005B/2202